CONFIRMATION
GETTING SERIOUS

7 Fundamentals in the Christian Faith

SERENDIPITY HOUSE / BOX 1012 / LITTLETON, CO 80160
TOLL FREE 1-800-525-9563 / www.serendipityhouse.com
© 1996 Serendipity House. All Rights Reserved.

99 00 01 02 / **YTH series•CHG** / 6 5 4 3

Contents: 7 Sessions

1 God the Father   5
Scripture Passage
Creation Story / Genesis 2
Team Building Goal
Team Sign-Up

2 Jesus Christ   11
Scripture Passage
Birth Story / Matthew 1:18–25
Team Building Goal
Learning to Share

3 Holy Spirit   17
Scripture Passage
Pentecost Foretold / Acts 1 and 2
Team Building Goal
Going Deeper

4 Church Universal   23
Scripture Passage
Early Church / Acts 2:42–47
Team Building Goal
Affirmation

5 Forgiveness of Sins   29
Scripture Passage
Crucifixion / Matthew 27:45–55
Team Building Goal
Getting Personal

6 Resurrection of the Body   35
Scripture Passage
Resurrection Story / Matthew 28:1–15
Team Building Goal
Learning to Care

7 Life Everlasting   41
Scripture Passage
Nicodemus / John 3:1–21
Team Building Goal
Team Celebration

BEFORE ... DURING ... AFTER

Progress Report

We will check to see where you are three times during this course—at the end of the ...

- First session
- Fourth session
- Seventh session

If you had a complete physical, mental, relational and spiritual check-up at the Mayo Clinic by doctors in these fields, what would they conclude about you? Record your pulse in each of these areas by putting a dot on the line below to indicate how you see yourself—1 being POOR and 10 being EXCELLENT health.

Physically: I am feeling good physically. I stay in shape by exercising regularly and eating right. I sleep well and enjoy life. Physically, I am ...

Poor ———————————————————————— Excellent
    1 2 3 4 5 6 7 8 9 10

Mentally: I am feeling good about myself. I build myself up. I have some God-given abilities. I am aware of my strengths. I like who I am. Mentally, I am ...

Poor ———————————————————————— Excellent
    1 2 3 4 5 6 7 8 9 10

Relationally: I am feeling good about sharing myself with others. I make friends well. I deal with conflict. I reach out, care and forgive. Relationally, I am ...

Poor ———————————————————————— Excellent
    1 2 3 4 5 6 7 8 9 10

Spiritually: I am feeling good about my relationship with God. I am getting my spiritual life together, putting God first. Spiritually, I am ...

Poor ———————————————————————— Excellent
    1 2 3 4 5 6 7 8 9 10

Love the Lord your God with all your heart and with all your soul and with all your mind and with all your strength. Love your neighbor as yourself.

Mark 12:30–31

SESSION 1
God the Father

LEADER:
Before you start, read A Word to the Youth Leaders, on page 46.

CROWD BREAKER

LEADER:
Pass out books. Explain teamwork principle. Explain diagrams on page 46 and theory behind 2's, 4's and 8's. Read Introduction out loud and break into teams of 8—preferably with a leader assigned to each team. Then, pair off in 2's for the Conservation Starter. (If you have less than six youth, you may want to stay together for the entire meeting.)

CONVERSATION STARTER

LEADER:
Call time after 15 minutes and move to Bible Study.

See *Coach's Book*.

Introduction: Welcome to the team. Your youth leader has probably explained how this program works and the importance of teamwork. We would like to reinforce what this person has already said.

    This program works like a sports training camp. In each session you will be put through a series of exercises—starting out with groups of 2; then moving into groups of 4, and finally groups of 8. The reason for this is to give you a chance to participate in the size of group that is most suitable for what you are doing. The purpose of this program is to let you discuss what you believe about the seven major statements in the Apostles' Creed—the foundation of the Christian faith. At the end of this session, you will have a chance to decide on the ground rules for your group—especially the ground rule of respect for each other's opinions. In this session, you will discuss the first statement in the Apostles' Creed: *"I believe in God, the Father Almighty, creator of heaven and earth ..."*

Groups of 2 / 15 minutes

How I See Myself. To get started, get together with one other person from your team and have fun describing how you see yourself to one another. On the first category, both of you finish the sentence below by choosing one of the two options on the first line. Then, go to the next category and both finish the sentence again. Have fun.

I See Myself As A ...

1. talker . . . . listener
2. doer. . . . . thinker
3. Porsche . . . . Jeep
4. pitcher . . . . catcher
5. sprinter . . . . long-distance runner
6. wallflower . . . . sunflower
7. first and 10 . . . . goal to go
8. deep, mysterious ocean . . . . gentle-flowing stream
9. rock music . . . . country music
10. cultured pearl . . . . diamond in the rough

BIBLE STUDY

LEADER:
Put two groups of 2 together to make groups of 4. Rearrange chairs. Read Introduction and Scripture aloud. Save 30 minutes for the last part—Caring Time.

Groups of 4 / 15–30 minutes

Where It All Began. The Bible Study time in this program is a little different from the usual Bible study because the purpose of the course is different. The purpose of this course is to get to know each other and become a team that supports one another in your spiritual walk.

For this reason, the Bible Study is designed around a two-part questionnaire: (1) **Looking Into the Story**—about the Bible story, and (2) **My Own Story**—about your own life. The questionnaire has multiple-choice options to choose from and there are no right or wrong answers—because the purpose is not to test your knowledge of the Bible. The purpose is to help you talk about yourself, using the Bible story as a springboard. We recommend that you move into groups of 4 for the Bible Study time so that everyone can participate and finish the discussion in 30 minutes. In the last 30 minutes of this session, you will get back together with your team of 8 and decide on the ground rules for your group. Be sure to save enough time for this.

Now, let's start with the first statement in the Apostles' Creed: "*I believe in God, the Father Almighty, creator of heaven and earth ...*" Move into groups of 4 and listen to the Scripture passage.

⁴This is the account of the heavens and the earth when they were created.

When the Lord God made the earth and the heavens—⁵and no shrub of the field had yet appeared on the earth and no plant of the field had yet sprung up, for the Lord God had not sent rain on the earth and there was no man to work the ground, ⁶but streams came up from the earth and watered the whole surface of the ground—⁷the Lord God formed the man from the dust of the ground and breathed into his nostrils the breath of life, and the man became a living being.

⁸Now the Lord God had planted a garden in the east, in Eden; and there he put the man he had formed. ⁹And the Lord God made all kinds of trees grow out of the ground—trees that were pleasing to the eye and good for food. In the middle of the garden were the tree of life and the tree of the knowledge of good and evil.

¹⁰A river watering the garden flowed from Eden; from there it was separated into four headwaters. ¹¹The name of the first is the Pishon; it winds through the entire land of Havilah, where there is gold. ¹²(The gold of that land is good; aromatic resin and onyx are also there.) ¹³The name of the second river is the Gihon; it winds through the entire land of Cush. ¹⁴The name of the third river is the Tigris; it runs along the east side of Asshur. And the fourth river is the Euphrates.

¹⁵The Lord God took the man and put him in the Garden of Eden to work it and take care of it. ¹⁶And the Lord God commanded the man, "You are free to eat from any tree in the garden; ¹⁷but you must not eat from the tree of the knowledge of good and evil, for when you eat of it you will surely die."

¹⁸The Lord God said, "It is not good for the man to be alone. I will make a helper suitable for him."

[19]Now the Lord God had formed out of the ground all the beasts of the field and all the birds of the air. He brought them to the man to see what he would name them; and whatever the man called each living creature, that was its name. [20]So the man gave names to all the livestock, the birds of the air and all the beasts of the field.

But for Adam no suitable helper was found. [21]So the Lord God caused the man to fall into a deep sleep; and while he was sleeping, he took one of the man's ribs and closed up the place with flesh. [22]Then the Lord God made a woman from the rib he had taken out of the man, and he brought her to the man.

[23]The man said,

"This is now bone of my bones
and flesh of my flesh;
she shall be called 'woman,'
for she was taken out of man."

[24]For this reason a man will leave his father and mother and be united to his wife, and they will become one flesh.

[25]The man and his wife were both naked, and they felt no shame.

Genesis 2:4–25

Looking Into the Story: In groups of 4, let one person answer question #1, the next person answer question #2, etc. around your group. Remember, there are no right or wrong answers, so feel free to speak up.

1. If you could have a snapshot showing just one moment in this creation story, what would it be?
   - ❏ when Adam came to life
   - ❏ a wide-angle view of the unspoiled Garden of Eden
   - ❏ the tree of the knowledge of good and evil
   - ❏ when Eve came to life
   - ❏ when Adam and Eve first saw each other—how ROMANTIC!

2. If you had to boil down this story into a few words, what would they be?
   - ❏ God made the whole enchilada.
   - ❏ Life had to start from somewhere—and that was God.
   - ❏ The man formed from dust has God's fingerprints all over him.
   - ❏ God made people to live in relationships.

3. What would you say is the most interesting thing about this story?
   - ❏ that God made us out of dirt—and now I have to take a bath every day!
   - ❏ that life came from the breath of God
   - ❏ that animals were not sufficient companions—me, I like my dog!
   - ❏ that woman was made out of man, and now man comes out of woman
   - ❏ that the man and woman were naked and were not embarrassed

4. What is the most convincing argument for the existence of God to you?
   - ❏ the harmony in the universe—the stars in the heavens
   - ❏ the beauty in the universe—from a tiny flower to the magnificent mountains
   - ❏ the longing that we have for meaning—the "God-shaped" vacuum in our lives
   - ❏ that every effect must have a cause, and so we need a "first cause" that was not in turn caused by something before it
   - ❏ that our moral sense must have come from one greater than humankind, since people are so often *not* moral

My Own Story: Note how the instructions shift on the second half of the questionnaire. Take question #1 and let everyone answer. Then, take question #2 and go around again, etc. through the questions.

1. Who is the person or people in your life that shaped you and influenced your early spiritual development?
   - ❏ my parent(s)
   - ❏ my grandparent(s)
   - ❏ Sunday School teacher
   - ❏ neighbor
   - ❏ coach
   - ❏ close friend
   - ❏ scoutmaster
   - ❏ uncle/aunt
   - ❏ pastor
   - ❏ youth leader
   - ❏ teacher
   - ❏ brother/sister

2. Who is like a "father" or "father figure" to you right now?
   - ❏ my father/stepfather
   - ❏ my friend's father
   - ❏ my coach/scoutmaster
   - ❏ a teacher at school I am close to
   - ❏ my mother
   - ❏ my uncle/aunt
   - ❏ my older brother/sister
   - ❏ I don't have anyone like that.

3. How do you feel about being in this course and talking about your faith and your relationship with God?
   - ❏ scared
   - ❏ a little funny
   - ❏ I'm not the talking type.
   - ❏ No problem, these are my friends.
   - ❏ stupid
   - ❏ okay, but ...
   - ❏ I'll let you know later.

4. If you go into this program about developing your faith, what do you want to have understood at the beginning?
   - ❏ Anything that is shared in the group is kept in confidence.
   - ❏ I can say "I pass" anytime I want.
   - ❏ We are all in this together—no spectators in this game.
   - ❏ Don't try to push religion on me.
   - ❏ We will respect each other.
   - ❏ This is not a study course where you feel stupid if you don't know a whole lot about the Bible.
   - ❏ other:_____

CARING TIME

LEADER:
If you have more than 12 youth, form groups of 8 by bringing two groups of 4 together. This group of 8 will stay together for the rest of this program—and meet together at the beginning and at the close of each session.

LEADER:
Bring all of the teams back together to do Step 3—particularly reinforcing the commitment to be present every session. Close the meeting with Step 4—prayer partners.

Groups of 8 / 30 minutes

 Team Sign-Up. Now is the time to decide what you want to get out of this course. For yourself. For your team. And for you to agree on the ground rules for teamwork. Follow these four steps.

Step 1: Check-In. Turn to page 3 and let everyone on your team explain where they are right now in these areas of their life. (You will have a chance to retake this test at the close of the course to see where you have grown.)

Step 2: Expectations. Give everyone a chance to share the top two things they would like to get out of this course, using the list below:

- ❐ to have fun
- ❐ to get closer as a youth group
- ❐ to hang out with my friends
- ❐ to reach out to other kids at school
- ❐ to talk about the real stuff in my life
- ❐ to get to know the Bible
- ❐ to grow in my faith
- ❐ other:_____

Step 3: Ground Rules. What are a couple of things on the list below that you would like to include in the ground rules for being in this course? See if you can agree on these.

- ❐ **ATTENDANCE:** I will be at all six remaining sessions.
- ❐ **OPENNESS:** I will share my thoughts and feelings openly each week.
- ❐ **CONFIDENTIALITY:** I will keep anything that is said at the meetings in confidence.
- ❐ **PRAYER:** I will pray for the others on my team.
- ❐ **REACH OUT:** I will invite others to join our group.
- ❐ **SERVICE:** I would like to see our team commit to a mission project at the close of this course.
- ❐ **CELEBRATION:** I would like to see us end this course together with a party or retreat.
- ❐ **ACCOUNTABILITY:** I would like to see us report in each week on our spiritual walk with Christ.

Step 4: Prayer Partner. Within your team, choose one or two others to conclude this meeting, and every meeting for the next six sessions, with a time of prayer. Before you pray, share how you are feeling, and how you want your prayer partner to pray for you this week. Then, call during the week to ask, "How's it going?"

SESSION 2
Jesus Christ

CROWD BREAKER

See *Coach's Book.*

CONVERSATION STARTER

LEADER:
Recap the last session. Repeat the teamwork principles. Ask teams of 8 to divide into groups of 2—not the same person as last session.

Groups of 2 / 15 minutes

Quiz Show. In the last session you talked about your expectations for this course and set the ground rules for your group. In this session, you will discuss what you believe about the person of Jesus Christ.

To get started, get together with one other person from your team (not the same person as last session) and play this quiz game. It is played like a typical quiz show. One of you will read the questions and your partner will try to guess your answer before you explain. If they guess right, your partner circles the money won.

When you have finished, reverse the roles and your partner reads the questions and you guess. The person with the most money at the end WINS. Remember, let your partner guess before you answer the question.

For $1: In music, I am closer to:
a. country   b. rock

For $2: I feel the most comfortable wearing:
a. dress clothes
b. casual clothes
c. grubbies

For $3: I would prefer a:
a. luxury car—10 mpg
b. sports car—20 mpg
c. economy car—30 mpg
d. tiny car—40 mpg

For $4: My preference would be to marry someone:
a. rich
b. famous
c. generous
d. beautiful/handsome
e. with a great personality

For $5: For a job, I would choose:
a. pickle inspector at processing plant
b. complaint officer at department store
c. bedpan changer at hospital
d. garbage collector
e. bus driver for junior high camp

For $6: I would choose for a vacation:
a. one-day shopping spree
b. two days at Disney World
c. three days at seashore resort
d. four days camping in open air
e. five days to rest at home

For $7: I would choose a life full of:
a. happiness
b. adventure
c. riches

BIBLE STUDY

LEADER
Combine two groups of 2 to make groups of 4. Read Introduction and Scripture. Call time 20 minutes before closing time.

Groups of 4 / 15–30 minutes

Lowly Beginnings. The second statement in the Apostles' Creed is: "*I believe in Jesus Christ, his only Son, our Lord. He was conceived by the power of the Holy Spirit and born of the virgin Mary. He suffered under Pontius Pilate, was crucified, died, and was buried. He descended into hell. On the third day he rose again. He ascended into heaven, and is seated at the right hand of the Father. He will come again to judge the living and the dead.*"

In the Bible study, you are going to focus on the events surrounding the birth of Jesus. The questionnaire has two parts: (1) **Looking Into the Story**—about the Bible story, and (2) **My Own Story**—about your own story. The multiple-choice options to each question will give you a chance to choose and there are no right or wrong answers, so feel free to express your opinion. Be sure to save the last 20 minutes in the session to get back together with your team to debrief what you have learned. Now, move into groups of 4 and listen to the Bible story.

[18]This is how the birth of Jesus Christ came about: His mother Mary was pledged to be married to Joseph, but before they came together, she was found to be with child through the Holy Spirit. [19]Because Joseph her husband was a righteous man and did not want to expose her to public disgrace, he had in mind to divorce her quietly.

[20]But after he had considered this, an angel of the Lord appeared to him in a dream and said, "Joseph son of David, do not be afraid to take Mary home as your wife, because what is conceived in her is from the Holy Spirit. [21]She will give birth to a son, and you are to give him the name Jesus, because he will save his people from their sins."

[22]All this took place to fulfill what the Lord had said through the prophet: [23]"The virgin will be with child and will give birth to a son, and they will call him Immanuel"—which means, "God with us."

[24]When Joseph woke up, he did what the angel of the Lord had commanded him and took Mary home as his wife. [25]But he had no union with her until she gave birth to a son. And he gave him the name Jesus.
Matthew 1:18–25

Looking Into the Story: In groups of 4, let one person answer question #1, the next person answer question #2, etc. around the group.

1. If you had been Mary when she found out she was pregnant, what would be the first thing to pop into your mind?
   ❒ No one will believe me, especially Joseph.
   ❒ What will the kids at school say?
   ❒ My parents are going to kick me out!
   ❒ Surely God must know what he's doing.

2. If you had been Joseph, her fiancé, what would be the first thing to come into your mind?
   - ❐ It must have been that party she went to without me!
   - ❐ What will the kids at school say?
   - ❐ What can I do to get back at her?
   - ❐ She's never lied to me before—maybe she's telling the truth.
   - ❐ Surely God must know what he's doing.

3. Why do you think God chose a teenage mother from a poor family in a little town to bring his Son into the world?
   - ❐ He wanted to identify with all the other kids born to teenagers.
   - ❐ He wanted a mother with the energy to keep up with Jesus.
   - ❐ That's when people had kids back then.
   - ❐ It was like showing the devil he could beat him "with his hands tied behind his back."

4. How do you think Joseph and Mary felt about being parents to a child God said would "save his people from their sins"?
   - ❐ overwhelmed
   - ❐ inadequate
   - ❐ happy to be part of it all
   - ❐ proud and egotistical

My Own Story: Note how the instructions for sharing change. Take question #1 and let everyone in your group answer the question. Then, go around again on question #2, etc.

1. If you asked this question: Who is Jesus Christ?—what would these people say? Put a symbol next to their view:

   TV = Jesus portrayed on TELEVISION
   PS = Jesus portrayed in PUBLIC SCHOOL
   F = Jesus as seen by my FRIENDS at school
   P = Jesus as seen by my PARENTS
   M = MY view of Jesus
   5 = MY view of Jesus FIVE years ago

   ___ greatest man who ever lived   ___ close friend
   ___ saint (someone I can never be)   ___ stained glass window
   ___ social revolutionary   ___ life giver
   ___ the Force (as in *Star Wars*)   ___ Lord and Savior
   ___ true God and true man   ___ preacher against fun
   ___ holy man (more spiritual than real) ___ a nice guy
   ___ founder of Christianity   ___ a swear word

2. When did Jesus become a warm person to you—more than just a name?
   - ❐ a few years ago
   - ❐ when I gave my life to him
   - ❐ only recently
   - ❐ I'm not sure about that.
   - ❐ He has always been a warm person to me.

3. How would you describe your relationship with Jesus right now in sports terms?
   - ❐ suiting up
   - ❐ sitting on the bench
   - ❐ playing "catch up"
   - ❐ waiting for the game to start
   - ❐ trying to figure out the game plan
   - ❐ worn out
   - ❐ giving it all I've got
   - ❐ at half time
   - ❐ on the injury list

4. In all honesty, what difference does Jesus make in your everyday life?
   - ❐ a great deal
   - ❐ quite a bit
   - ❐ some
   - ❐ not a whole lot
   - ❐ none at all

5. How does Jesus and your relationship with Jesus influence the decisions you make every day in these areas? Pick a number from 1 to 10—1 being NO INFLUENCE and 10 being BIG INFLUENCE.

   FRIENDS: choosing the people to run around with:

   1   2   3   4   5   6   7   8   9   10

   DATING: choosing the people to go out with:

   1   2   3   4   5   6   7   8   9   10

   LEISURE TIME: what to do with my spare time:

   1   2   3   4   5   6   7   8   9   10

   GRADES: doing my best in school:

   1   2   3   4   5   6   7   8   9   10

   FITNESS: keeping in shape:

   1   2   3   4   5   6   7   8   9   10

   SEX: keeping my body as the "temple of God":

   1   2   3   4   5   6   7   8   9   10

   JUSTICE: standing up for what I know is right:

   1   2   3   4   5   6   7   8   9   10

   SELF-ACCEPTANCE: believing in myself:

   1   2   3   4   5   6   7   8   9   10

CARING TIME

LEADER:
Bring teams back together for Step 1 and 2. Then, Step 3 with prayer partners for this course.

Groups of 8 / 15–20 minutes

Team Check-In: How's It Going? After two sessions in this program, stop the camera and evaluate what you think about the program ... and what you would like to change. Regather with your team and go over the questions together. Be sure to save the last few minutes to be with your prayer partner (Step 3).

Step 1: Check Your Pulse. What do you appreciate most about this course? Go around and let everyone share one or two things.

___ fun times
___ studying the Bible
___ close relationships
___ feeling like I belong
___ sharing our problems
___ praying for each other
___ reaching out to others
___ other:_____

Step 2: I Wish. If you could have one wish for this program, what would it be? Finish the sentence, "I wish we could have ..."

___ more sharing about each other
___ more time for Bible Study
___ more fun
___ more reaching out
___ more special events
___ less joking around
___ less gossip
___ less study
___ other:_____

Step 3: Prayer Partner. Get together with the prayer partner you started with last week, and describe the last seven days in your life as a weather report. Then, close in prayer for each other. Finish the sentence, "This past week has been ..."

❏ blue sky, bright sunshine all week long—NO PROBLEMS
❏ partly cloudy most of the week—A FEW PROBLEMS
❏ severe storms all week long
❏ mixed—some days sunny, some days cloudy
❏ warming trend—getting better
❏ tornado/hurricane—DISASTERS!
❏ other:_____

15

SESSION 3
Holy Spirit

CROWD BREAKER

See *Coach's Book*.

CONVERSATION STARTER

Groups of 2 / 15 minutes

Our Fantasy World. The Christian life can get discouraging at times, especially when tragedy strikes. In this session, you are going to see what happened to the disciples at the lowest moment in their lives.

To get started in this session, get together with one other person from your team (someone new) and interview each other using the questions below.

If you have time left over, respond to what you heard by finishing the sentences under the word FEEDBACK. Now, pair off with one other person and have fun:

INTERVIEW QUESTIONS:

1. If you could marry a famous movie star or sports hero, who would you choose?

2. If you could have a dream car given to you, what would you choose?

3. If you could join a circus, what would you like to be?

4. If you had unlimited money to blow on one glorious vacation, where would you go and what would you do?

5. If you could live at any time in history, what period would you choose to live in?

6. If you could live in any place in the world, where would you like to live?

Feedback: Finish these sentences about your partner.

1. The thing I especially liked about your fantasy world was ...

2. I think we are a lot alike in our ...

17

BIBLE STUDY

Groups of 4 / 15–30 minutes

People on Fire. The third statement in the Apostles' Creed is: *"I believe in the Holy Spirit."*

We are going to look at three places in Acts where the Holy Spirit is promised, the Holy Spirit comes, and the Holy Spirit is explained. The questionnaire is in two parts: (1) **Looking Into the Story**—about the Scripture, and (2) **My Own Story**—about your own experience.

Be sure to save the last 20 minutes for the Caring Time. Now, move into groups of 4 and listen to the Scripture.

⁶So when they met together, they asked him, "Lord, are you at this time going to restore the kingdom to Israel?"
⁷He said to them: "It is not for you to know the times or dates the Father has set by his own authority. ⁸But you will receive power when the Holy Spirit comes on you; and you will be my witnesses in Jerusalem, and in all Judea and Samaria, and to the ends of the earth."
⁹After he said this, he was taken up before their very eyes, and a cloud hid him from their sight. ...

2 When the day of Pentecost came, they were all together in one place. ²Suddenly a sound like the blowing of a violent wind came from heaven and filled the whole house where they were sitting. ³They saw what seemed to be tongues of fire that separated and came to rest on each of them. ⁴All of them were filled with the Holy Spirit and began to speak in other tongues as the Spirit enabled them. ...
¹⁴Then Peter stood up with the Eleven, raised his voice and addressed the crowd: "Fellow Jews and all of you who live in Jerusalem, let me explain this to you; listen carefully to what I say. ¹⁵These men are not drunk, as you suppose. It's only nine in the morning! ¹⁶No, this is what was spoken by the prophet Joel:
¹⁷" 'In the last days, God says,
   I will pour out my Spirit on all people.
Your sons and daughters will prophesy,
   your young men will see visions,
   your old men will dream dreams.

Acts 1:6–9; 2:1–4,14–17

Looking Into the Story: In groups of 4, let one person answer question #1, the next person answer question #2 ... etc. around your group.

1. If I had been present with the disciples when Christ was taken up to heaven, I would have ...
   ❑ immediately taken the story to *The National Enquirer*
   ❑ wondered who spiked my cola
   ❑ cried and felt abandoned
   ❑ ran around telling anyone who would believe me
   ❑ just kept quiet so nobody would think I was crazy

2. What would you say was the most impressive evidence of the Holy Spirit that is referred to in this passage?
   - ❏ the sudden mysterious wind
   - ❏ the tongues of fire that came to rest on each of them
   - ❏ people speaking in other languages without taking a class!
   - ❏ the seeing of visions and dreams

3. What do the images of wind and fire, used for the Holy Spirit's presence, suggest to you most strongly?
   - ❏ unpredictability—Like wind and fire are unpredictable, so you cannot always predict what God will do next through the Spirit.
   - ❏ power—Wind and fire are two of nature's most powerful forces, and remind us of the power of the Spirit.
   - ❏ invisibility—Like the wind and the heat of a fire, you cannot always see the Spirit at work.
   - ❏ change—Wind suggests changes are coming and the Holy Spirit brings change to the world.
   - ❏ warmth—Fire brings warmth, and the Spirit brings the warmth of love.

My Own Story: Note how the sharing instructions change. Take question #1 and let everyone answer the question. Then, take question #2 and go around again, etc. through the questions.

1. Had you been present on the day of Pentecost, what would have been your main feeling when it was all over?
   - ❏ That was a once-in-a-lifetime experience.
   - ❏ I hope that wasn't a once-in-a-lifetime experience.
   - ❏ If the Spirit is that powerful, there's no problem I can't face.
   - ❏ Give us five days and we'll take the world!
   - ❏ Nobody at school is going to understand this!

2. When it comes to particular situations, how would you stand up? Put an "X" on the line somewhere in between PANIC BUTTON and SUPER COOL. For example:

FAMILY: Getting along with everybody:

_____
PANIC BUTTON   **SUPER COOL**

GRADES: Living up to others' expectations:

_____
PANIC BUTTON   **SUPER COOL**

FRIENDS: Being accepted by those who count:

_____
PANIC BUTTON   **SUPER COOL**

FUTURE: Feeling secure in God's hands:

PANIC BUTTON   **SUPER COOL**

3. In comparison to what the disciples experienced when the Holy Spirit came upon them, how would you describe your own experience with the Holy Spirit?
   - ❏ much more tame
   - ❏ different, but just as real
   - ❏ very similar to theirs
   - ❏ something I can't explain

4. The following qualities from Galatians 5 are called the "fruit of the Spirit." Evaluate your life by circling a number from 1 to 10—1 being VERY low and 10 being VERY high—on each of the "fruit" in the list. Then share which fruit you marked as highest and lowest. Lastly, have each person listen while the others share which fruit they see as that person's highest.

But the fruit of the Spirit is love, joy, peace, patience, kindness, goodness, faithfulness, gentleness and self-control.

LOVE: I am quick to sense the needs of my friends, classmates and family; I try to respond as Christ would in giving of myself.
    1   2   3   4   5   6   7   8   9   10

JOY: I can celebrate life even in the midst of pain and confusion because of my faith in Christ.
    1   2   3   4   5   6   7   8   9   10

PEACE: I have a quiet inner confidence in God's care of my life that keeps me from feeling uptight and nervous.
    1   2   3   4   5   6   7   8   9   10

PATIENCE: I have a staying power that helps me to handle frustration and conflict without blowing my stack when people irritate me.
    1   2   3   4   5   6   7   8   9   10

KINDNESS: I act toward my friends, classmates and family as I want them to act toward me—warm, considerate, generous with praise—always trying to see the best in others.
    1   2   3   4   5   6   7   8   9   10

GOODNESS: I have a desire to live a clean life, to set a good example by my conduct wherever I am; I want to be God's man/woman.
    1   2   3   4   5   6   7   8   9   10

FAITHFULNESS: I stick to my word; I stand up for my friends; I can be counted on to stay firm in my commitments to God and others.
    1   2   3   4   5   6   7   8   9   10

GENTLENESS: I have an inner strength that permits me to be gentle in my relationships; I am aware of my own abilities without having to make a show of them.

1   2   3   4   5   6   7   8   9   10

SELF-CONTROL: I am learning to discipline my time, energy and desires to reflect my spiritual values and priorities.

1   2   3   4   5   6   7   8   9   10

CARING TIME

Groups of 8 / 15–20 minutes

How Do You Feel About Your Team? You have been with your team now for three sessions. Take your pulse on how you feel about your group. Steps 1 and 2 are for your team together. Step 3 is with your prayer partner.

Step 1: Report In. If you could compare your involvement in this program to the diagram below, where would you be?

- In the grandstand—for spectators—just looking on
- On the bench—on the team—but not playing
- On the playing field—where the action is
- In the showers—on the injury list

Step 2: Teamwork. How would you describe the way you work together as a team?

- We're playing more like individuals than like a team.
- We're just starting to trust each other.
- Our teamwork is awkward—but improving.
- We're on a roll—like a championship team.

Step 3: Prayer Partner. Get together with your prayer partner and check to see how last week went. Then, spend a little time in prayer for each other. Start off by picking a number from 1 to 10—1 being TERRIBLE and 10 being GREAT—to describe how last week went.

SESSION 4
Church Universal

CROWD BREAKER

See *Coach's Book*.

CONVERSATION STARTER

Groups of 2 / 15 minutes

My Favorite Things. What are your likes? What are your dislikes? This is one way of finding out about your personality.

To get started, pair off with one other person from your team (someone that you do *not* know very well) and work together on this exercise.

Read over the list below and choose the top five things you like to do. Then, compare your list with your partner's list.

MY TOP FIVE   MY PARTNER'S TOP FIVE

_____Sports   _____
_____Watching TV   _____
_____Hiking/biking   _____
_____Listening to music   _____
_____Shopping   _____
_____Talking on the phone   _____
_____Working out   _____
_____Spending time alone   _____
_____Spending time with friends   _____
_____Playing with my computer   _____
_____Reading   _____
_____Working on my car/bike   _____
_____Going to the shore/mountains   _____
_____Doing crossword puzzles   _____
_____Going to parties   _____
_____Working on my hobby   _____
_____Playing a musical instrument   _____
_____Collecting baseball cards/posters   _____
_____Decorating my room   _____

BIBLE STUDY

Groups of 4 / 15–30 minutes

 A Really Tight Group. The fourth statement in the Apostles' Creed is: *"I believe in ... the holy catholic Church, the communion of saints."*

The word "catholic" means "universal" ... so you could say universal church if you wish. The Bible passage for this session comes right after the Scripture for the last session. In fact it describes what happened on the day of Pentecost when so many came into the church that they decided to gather in homes to care for each other.

The questionnaire is in two parts: (1) **Looking Into the Story**—about their experience, and (2) **My Own Story**—about your experience. Be sure to save the last 20 minutes of the session for the Caring Time. Now, move into groups of 4 and listen to the Scripture.

⁴²They devoted themselves to the apostles' teaching and to the fellowship, to the breaking of bread and to prayer. ⁴³Everyone was filled with awe, and many wonders and miraculous signs were done by the apostles. ⁴⁴All the believers were together and had everything in common. ⁴⁵Selling their possessions and goods, they gave to anyone as he had need. ⁴⁶Every day they continued to meet together in the temple courts. They broke bread in their homes and ate together with glad and sincere hearts, ⁴⁷praising God and enjoying the favor of all the people. And the Lord added to their number daily those who were being saved.

Acts 2:42–47

Looking Into the Story: In groups of 4, let one person answer question #1, the next person answer question #2, etc. around the group. Remember, there are no right or wrong answers, so speak up.

1. Why do you think these first Christians got together almost every day?
   ❐ They loved to eat.
   ❐ They wanted to talk about their new life.
   ❐ They had a lot of needs.
   ❐ They had a lot to learn.
   ❐ They didn't have anything else to do.

2. How would you describe the atmosphere when they got together? (choose two or three)
   ❐ like a zoo   ❐ life-changing
   ❐ fun   ❐ predictable
   ❐ exciting   ❐ depressing
   ❐ boring   ❐ close
   ❐ status quo   ❐ noisy
   ❐ warm   ❐ caring

3. What made the early church so appealing that thousands wanted to get in?
   - ❏ the food
   - ❏ great preaching
   - ❏ the fun times
   - ❏ great advertising
   - ❏ their openness to others
   - ❏ the crazy love they had for each other
   - ❏ the unexpected things that happened

4. How do you think they felt about their church?
   - ❏ It must have been pretty important to them.
   - ❏ It was all they had.
   - ❏ They could take it or leave it.
   - ❏ It must have been like the last day at camp—so close that you felt like one big happy family.

My Own Story: Note how the sharing instructions change. Take question #1 and let everyone answer the question. Then, take question #2 and go around again, etc. through the questions.

1. As you think back, what is the closest you have come to experiencing the kind of close fellowship that the early church experienced?
   - ❏ I think our youth group is something like this.
   - ❏ I was on an athletic team that was really close.
   - ❏ I have a few close friends like this.
   - ❏ I have never experienced anything like this.

2. If you had to rank your own youth group or group that you are in now on the six areas that are described in the early church, what would you say? In your group, read the first area below and let everyone call out a number from 1 to 10—1 being VERY WEAK and 10 being VERY STRONG in that area.

   SPIRITUAL FORMATION: *"They devoted themselves to the apostles' teaching and to the fellowship, to the breaking of bread and to prayer."*

   We have given PRIORITY to studying the Scripture, to learning more about our faith and to praying for one another.
   1   2   3   4   5   6   7   8   9   10

   HEALING: *"Everyone was filled with awe, and many wonders and miraculous signs were done by the apostles."*

   We have seen healing take place in our lives and in our relationships with one another, our families and our friends.
   1   2   3   4   5   6   7   8   9   10

SPIRITUAL CARETAKING: *"All the believers were together and had everything in common. Selling their possessions and goods, they gave to anyone as he had need."*

We look after each other. If someone has a need, we do what we can to care for this person and meet their need.
1   2   3   4   5   6   7   8   9   10

CORPORATE WORSHIP: *"Every day they continued to meet together in the temple courts."*

We meet regularly for worship with the larger body of believers—to celebrate Christ's resurrection and his triumph over sin.
1   2   3   4   5   6   7   8   9   10

SUPPORT GROUPS: *"They broke bread in their homes and ate together with glad and sincere hearts, praising God and enjoying the favor of all the people."*

We meet regularly to support one another, study the Bible, share our needs and pray for one another.
1   2   3   4   5   6   7   8   9   10

NUMERICAL MULTIPLICATION: *"And the Lord added to their number daily those who were being saved."*

We keep our group open to new people and the Lord keeps bringing others to our meetings.
1   2   3   4   5   6   7   8   9   10

3. If you had to describe your own church or youth group with allegories, what would you say? Finish the sentence: *"I see our church more like a ..."*

   family . . . . club
   hospital . . . . outpatient clinic
   first and ten . . . . fourth and goal
   drive-in . . . . cafeteria

4. If you were the pastor of your church, how would you change things to make your church into more of a caring community—starting with your youth group?

CARING TIME

Groups of 8 / 15–20 minutes

 Mid-Course Affirmation. It's halftime. Time for a break. Get together with your team of 8 (or the whole group if you have 12 or less) and evaluate your experience so far.

Here are two options. The second option is more risky, but a lot more personal if you are comfortable with it.

Option 1: Halftime Progress Report. Turn to the Progress Report on page 3 and let everyone report any growth in their lives since being in this program.

Option 2: Appreciation Time. Ask one person on your team to sit in silence while the others share one thing that they have come to appreciate about this person. Finish one of these sentences:

Since being in your group, I have come to see you as ...

or

Since being in your group, I have come to appreciate you for your ...

After you have gone around your group on the first person, ask the next person to sit in silence while the others finish the sentence on this person ... etc. around the group.

This is called "strength bombardment" or "appreciation bombardment." You've done a lot of talking about yourself during this program. Now you will have a chance to hear what the others on your team have learned about you. Get set for a beautiful experience in AFFIRMATION.

If you don't know how to get started, look over the list below and pick out a word or two words that help describe what you see in this person ... and tell them so.

I SEE YOU AS VERY ...

loyal	nice	warm	crazy
peaceful	cheerful	dedicated	courageous
dependable	loving	gentle	special
daring	cool	kind	thoughtful
fun	sensitive	compassionate	energetic
open	prayerful	perceptive	encouraging
generous	spiritual	strong	beautiful
lovable	caring	sincere	persistent
friendly	together	playful	confident

SESSION 5
Forgiveness of Sins

CROWD BREAKER

See *Coach's Book*.

CONVERSATION STARTER

Groups of 2 / 15 minutes

My Last Will and Testament. This is going to be a heavy session, because you are going to talk about the death of Jesus Christ ... for the forgiveness of sins.

Get together with one other person from your team and discuss the funeral arrangements below, choosing from the multiple-choice options. Let your partner interview you.

HOW WOULD YOU CHOOSE TO DIE?
- ❒ prolong life as long as possible with support systems
- ❒ die naturally in a hospital with pain relievers if needed
- ❒ die at home without medical care—but with family

WHAT FUNERAL WOULD YOU CHOOSE?
- ❒ big funeral with lots of flowers
- ❒ small funeral, money to charity
- ❒ no funeral, just family at grave

WHAT WOULD YOU WANT ON YOUR TOMBSTONE?
- ❒ the words from my favorite song
- ❒ something about my life
- ❒ just my date of birth and death

HOW WOULD YOU LIKE TO BE REMEMBERED?
- ❒ someone who cared for people
- ❒ someone who loved God
- ❒ someone who lived life to the fullest

HOW WOULD YOU WANT YOUR BODY TREATED?
- ❒ cremated   ❒ given to science   ❒ buried intact

WHERE WOULD YOU LIKE YOUR MONEY TO GO?
- ❒ to my children   ❒ to a charity
- ❒ to a memorial in my honor

BIBLE STUDY

Groups of 4 / 15–30 minutes

A Dark Day. The fifth statement in the Apostles' Creed is: *"I believe in ... the forgiveness of sins."*

The Bible Study is about the crucifixion of Jesus Christ, because you can't talk about the forgiveness of sins without giving the explanation—that somebody had to pay the price. And that somebody had to be sinless. And that person was Jesus—"the Lamb of God." Your youth leader can help explain this further. Right now, you are going to look at the death of Jesus as a historical record. The questionnaire is in two parts: (1) **Looking Into the Story**—about the story in the Bible, and (2) **My Own Story**—about your own understanding of the story.

Be sure to save the last 20 minutes in the session to regather your team and debrief what you learned. Now, move into groups of 4 and listen to the story of the crucifixion of Christ.

⁴⁵From the sixth hour until the ninth hour darkness came over all the land. ⁴⁶About the ninth hour Jesus cried out in a loud voice, "Eloi, Eloi, lama sabachthani?"—which means, "My God, my God, why have you forsaken me?"

⁴⁷When some of those standing there heard this, they said, "He's calling Elijah."

⁴⁸Immediately one of them ran and got a sponge. He filled it with wine vinegar, put it on a stick, and offered it to Jesus to drink. ⁴⁹The rest said, "Now leave him alone. Let's see if Elijah comes to save him."

⁵⁰And when Jesus had cried out again in a loud voice, he gave up his spirit.

⁵¹At that moment the curtain of the temple was torn in two from top to bottom. The earth shook and the rocks split. ⁵²The tombs broke open and the bodies of many holy people who had died were raised to life. ⁵³They came out of the tombs, and after Jesus' resurrection they went into the holy city and appeared to many people.

⁵⁴When the centurion and those with him who were guarding Jesus saw the earthquake and all that had happened, they were terrified, and exclaimed, "Surely he was the Son of God!"

⁵⁵Many women were there, watching from a distance. They had followed Jesus from Galilee to care for his needs.

Matthew 27:45–55

Looking Into the Story: In groups of 4, let one person answer question #1, the next person answer question #2, etc. around the group.

1. If you were the editor of the *Jerusalem Times*, what headline would you pick to describe the events of the death of Christ?
   ❑ "Strange Darkness Descends"   ❑ "Earthquake Rocks City"
   ❑ "Dead People Reported Seen"   ❑ "Spiritual Leader Killed"
   ❑ "Temple Curtain Ruined"

2. With all of the supernatural signs that accompanied Jesus' death, why didn't more people believe?
   ❐ They figured it was all coincidental.
   ❐ They felt too guilty to realize what they had done.
   ❐ They thought it was all just a bad dream.
   ❐ They probably didn't know enough about Jesus to make the connection.

3. What is the significance of the fact that darkness came for three hours in the middle of the day when Jesus was crucified?
   ❐ There was probably an eclipse.
   ❐ The darkness of sin was being dealt with.
   ❐ Taking away life-giving light showed God's anger.
   ❐ The forces of evil were at the height of their power.
   ❐ God was so disgusted he didn't want anyone to see what was happening.

4. What caused Jesus to cry out, "My God, my God, why have you forsaken me?"
   ❐ the physical pain he was suffering
   ❐ the feeling that God had deserted him
   ❐ God really did turn his back on him at that moment.
   ❐ He thought the whole world had turned against him.
   ❐ He was angry at God.

5. What do you think the centurion (army officer), who here proclaims Jesus as the Son of God, did the next morning?
   ❐ figured he had let his fear get the best of him
   ❐ tried to forget all about it
   ❐ searched out Jesus' followers to find out more about Jesus
   ❐ asked God to forgive him for his role in Jesus' death
   ❐ other_____

6. How would you explain the significance of the death of Jesus Christ to one of your friends at school?
   ❐ God put up the "bail bond" to get people out of jail.
   ❐ Jesus became the substitute to pay for everybody's sin.
   ❐ God opened a charge account in my name—PAID in full.
   ❐ God gave me an AT&T credit card—dial direct anytime.

My Own Story: Note how the instructions change on discussing this part of the questionnaire. Take question #1 and let everyone answer the question. Then, go around again on question #2, etc. through the questions. Don't forget to save the last 20 minutes at the close for the Caring Time.

1. What would be most likely to make *you* proclaim publicly, in the presence of your friends, "Surely he was the Son of God!"?
   - ❐ a lot of scary signs, like those that happened that day
   - ❐ feeling forgiven for all the bad things I've done
   - ❐ seeing how badly my friends need Christ
   - ❐ No way I'd *ever* say such a thing!
   - ❐ I say it all the time already.

2. What remains a mystery to you about the death of Jesus?
   - ❐ why it was necessary
   - ❐ how God could let this happen to his son
   - ❐ why nobody came to his rescue
   - ❐ why his disciples didn't understand at the time

3. What are the results of God's forgiveness? Below are a series of big words that the Bible uses to describe the effects of the death of Jesus Christ. In your group, read one definition and let everyone call out a number from 1 to 10 to indicate how much you understand the meaning—1 being DON'T UNDERSTAND and 10 being UNDERSTAND COMPLETELY.

   I AM JUSTIFIED: *"Therefore, since we have been justified through faith, we have peace with God through our Lord Jesus Christ."*   *Romans 5:1*

   The sentence of death that was hanging over my head has been canceled because Jesus took my place on the cross ... and God marked my debt PAID.

   Don't understand   1   2   3   4   5   6   7   8   9   10   **Do understand**

   I AM RECONCILED: *"All this is from God, who reconciled us to himself through Christ and gave us the ministry of reconciliation."*   *2 Corinthians 5:18*

   My broken relationship with God because of sin has been rebuilt through the death of Jesus. My friendship with God is restored.

   Don't understand   1   2   3   4   5   6   7   8   9   10   **Do understand**

   I AM REDEEMED: *"In him we have redemption through his blood, the forgiveness of sins, in accordance with the riches of God's grace."*   *Ephesians 1:7*

   The payment for my sin has been paid by Jesus on the cross and I am free to serve my new master—Jesus Christ.

   Don't understand   1   2   3   4   5   6   7   8   9   10   **Do understand**

I AM TRANSFORMED: *"Therefore, if anyone is in Christ, he is a new creation; the old has gone, the new has come!"*

2 Corinthians 5:17

God has wiped the chalkboard clean. My sin has been erased. I get to start all over again—as if nothing had happened.

Don't understand   1   2   3   4   5   6   7   8   9   10   Do understand

4. How does it make you feel when you think about what God has done for you through the death of Jesus Christ on the cross?
   - ❒ bored
   - ❒ interested
   - ❒ grateful
   - ❒ I've heard all of this before.

CARING TIME

Groups of 8 / 15–20 minutes

Getting Personal. Here are two options to choose from to close this session.

Option 1: Follow the usual procedure. Regather as teams and report in on the session—what you learned—and spend some time in prayer with your prayer partner.

Option 2: Try a new form of sharing prayer requests and praying for one another. If you choose this option, here are the instructions.

1. Get together in groups of three. (Some groups may need to have four persons.)

2. Let one person share a prayer request by answering the question:

   How can we help you in prayer this week?

3. The other two respond to this prayer request in this way:

   • One person prays a prayer of *thanks* ...

   "God, I want to thank you for (name) ..."

   • The other person prays a prayer of *petition* ...

   "God, I ask your help for my friend (name), for ..."

4. When you have finished with the first person, let the next person share a request and the other two pray for this person.

   Remember, in your group of three, you start out by letting one person answer this question:

   How can we help you in prayer this week?

SESSION 6
The Resurrection of the Body

CROWD BREAKER

See *Coach's Book.*

CONVERSATION STARTER

Groups of 2 / 15 minutes

Sharing Dreams. Here's your chance to dream about your future. Get together with one other person from your team and interview each other on your future plans.

Below is a list of questions. Each of you have seven and a half minutes to interview your partner. You can choose as many or as few of the questions as you wish, but you only have seven and a half minutes. Then, your youth leader is going to call time and ask you to reverse roles. If you have time at the end, you can give your partner FEEDBACK from the interview—using the half-finished sentences at the bottom.

1. What would you like to be doing five years from now?
2. Where would you like to be living five years from now?
3. In 10 years, how much money would you like to be making?
4. What will it take for you to get where you want to be in 10 years?
5. What values will you look for in the person you will marry?
6. What spiritual commitment would you want this person to have?
7. How many children would you like to have? Boys or girls?
8. When are you going to allow them to start dating?
9. Are you going to send them to a private school or a public school?
10. Are you going to be more or less strict with your kids than your parents have been with you?
11. Will you get along better with your parent(s) when you leave home?
12. Will you invite your parent(s) to live with you when they get older, or will you have them go to a nursing home?

Feedback: Finish these two sentences about your partner.

1. As I listened to you talk about your dreams, I was reminded of the song or movie ...

2. The thing I appreciate about what you said was ...

BIBLE STUDY

Groups of 4 / 15–30 minutes

A New Day Dawns. The next statement in the Apostles' Creed is: *"I believe in ... the resurrection of the body."*

The phrase "the resurrection of the body" actually refers to the resurrection of Christians at the second coming of Jesus Christ. But this is in the future and we are not going to study a Scripture about this. We are going to study the story of the resurrection of Jesus Christ. The two are connected. If you believe in one, you believe in the other.

The questionnaire is in two parts: (1) **Looking Into the Story**—about the Bible story, and (2) **My Own Story**—about my understanding of the Bible story. Be sure to save the last 20 minutes in the session to regather as a team and debrief what you have learned. Now, move into groups of 4 and listen to the Bible story.

20 *After the Sabbath, at dawn on the first day of the week, Mary Magdalene and the other Mary went to look at the tomb.*
²There was a violent earthquake, for an angel of the Lord came down from heaven and, going to the tomb, rolled back the stone and sat on it. ³His appearance was like lightning, and his clothes were white as snow. ⁴The guards were so afraid of him that they shook and became like dead men.

⁵The angel said to the women, "Do not be afraid, for I know that you are looking for Jesus, who was crucified. ⁶He is not here; he has risen, just as he said. Come and see the place where he lay. ⁷Then go quickly and tell his disciples: 'He has risen from the dead and is going ahead of you into Galilee. There you will see him.' Now I have told you."

⁸So the women hurried away from the tomb, afraid yet filled with joy, and ran to tell his disciples. ⁹Suddenly Jesus met them. "Greetings," he said. They came to him, clasped his feet and worshiped him. ¹⁰Then Jesus said to them, "Do not be afraid. Go and tell my brothers to go to Galilee; there they will see me."

¹¹While the women were on their way, some of the guards went into the city and reported to the chief priests everything that had happened. ¹²When the chief priests had met with the elders and devised a plan, they gave the soldiers a large sum of money, ¹³telling them, "You are to say, 'His disciples came during the night and stole him away while we were asleep.' ¹⁴If this report gets to the governor, we will satisfy him and keep you out of trouble." ¹⁵So the soldiers took the money and did as they were instructed. And this story has been widely circulated among the Jews to this very day.
                                                                    Matthew 28:1–15

Looking Into the Story: In groups of 4, let one person answer question #1, the next person question #2, etc. around the group.

1. Why do you think Mary Magdalene and the other Mary went to the tomb on Easter morning?
   ❏ to pay their respect to the dead
   ❏ to bribe the guards into seeing Jesus' body one last time
   ❏ because they expected to see Jesus alive
   ❏ because they missed Jesus

2. When they found the stone rolled away and an angel sitting on it, how do you think they felt?
   ❏ scared to death
   ❏ confused—Where is Jesus?
   ❏ suspicious—Someone has taken the body.
   ❏ overcome with grief—I can't take any more heartache.
   ❏ overcome with joy—I knew he would come back as he said!

3. How do you think the women felt when Jesus suddenly met them?
   ❏ shocked   ❏ overjoyed
   ❏ afraid   ❏ full of praise

4. Why would the chief priests and the elders (politicians) want to spread the rumor that the disciples of Jesus came during the night and stole the body of Jesus?
   ❏ He was a threat to them.
   ❏ He might file charges against them for falsely accusing him.
   ❏ The Resurrection would prove that everything he said was true—he was the Son of God as he claimed.
   ❏ They saw him as a troublemaker, and they wanted to keep the peace.

My Own Story: Note how the instructions change now for sharing the second half of the questionnaire. Take question #1 and let everyone answer the question. Then, take question #2 and go around again, etc. through the questions. Be sure to save the last 20 minutes for the Caring Time.

1. When have you felt like these women felt when they found out Jesus was alive?
   ❏ when we came back to win "the big game"
   ❏ when my teacher allowed a re-test when I had flunked
   ❏ when I got back together again with a boyfriend/girlfriend
   ❏ when a loved one recovered from a bad illness
   ❏ when I found my pet after thinking he had disappeared for good

2. Have you ever attended the funeral of a Christian—someone that believed in the resurrection of Jesus and their own resurrection? What was it like?

3. What does this story say to you about your own death and life beyond it?
   ❏ God would raise his Son, but why would he bother with me?
   ❏ Hey, this is just a story—like Peter Pan and Aladdin.
   ❏ If God can raise Jesus, he can raise me.
   ❏ It's like the angel and Jesus told the woman: "Do not be afraid."

4. What do you do when you do not understand the resurrection of Jesus or your own resurrection?
   ❏ fall back on what the Bible says
   ❏ accept the teaching of my church
   ❏ go with what I was taught as a child
   ❏ accept it "by faith"—"I believe ... help my unbelief"
   ❏ other:_____

5. Here is a passage in the Bible about our resurrection from the dead. Read the Scripture out loud. Then, take the first phrase and let each one in your group call out a number to indicate how much you understand what it says from 1 to 10—1 being DON'T UNDERSTAND and 10 being COMPLETE UNDERSTANDING. The Scripture begins by answering the critics who say there will be no bodily resurrection.

   [12]But if it is preached that Christ has been raised from the dead, how can some of you say that there is no resurrection of the dead? [13]If there is no resurrection of the dead, then not even Christ has been raised. [14]And if Christ has not been raised, our preaching is useless and so is your faith. ...

   [20]But Christ has indeed been raised from the dead, the firstfruits of those who have fallen asleep. [21]For since death came through a man, the resurrection of the dead comes also through a man. [22]For as in Adam all die, so in Christ all will be made alive. [23]But each in his own turn: Christ, the firstfruits; then, when he comes, those who belong to him.   1 Cor. 15:12–14,20–23

   HOW DEATH GOT STARTED: Adam started a curse called sin that resulted in death for the entire human race.

   Don't understand   1   2   3   4   5   6   7   8   9   10   Do understand

   HOW JESUS TOOK CARE OF THE CURSE: Jesus took the place of all people when he suffered the consequences of sin in his own death.

   Don't understand   1   2   3   4   5   6   7   8   9   10   Do understand

   WHY JESUS HAD TO RAISE FROM THE DEAD: To prove that the curse of death was broken, Jesus rose from the dead.

   Don't understand   1   2   3   4   5   6   7   8   9   10   Do understand

WHEN CHRISTIANS WILL EXPERIENCE RESURRECTION: Christians who have already died, plus those who "belong to him" will one day be called to heaven at the second coming of Jesus.

Don't understand   1   2   3   4   5   6   7   8   9   10   Do understand

CARING TIME

Groups of 8 / 15–20 minutes

Learning to Care. You are nearly through with this course as a youth group. Next week, you will have a chance to celebrate and decide what you are going to do next.

To prepare for your last session together, take a few minutes right now and reflect on how you have changed during this course.

1. **Affirmation.** Go around and let everyone on your team answer one or more of the questions below. If you know each other fairly well, use this time to share how you have seen your teammates grow.

    - Where have you grown in your own life during this course?
    - Where have you seen growth in some of the others in your group during this course?
    - What have you liked most about the group during this course?

2. **Option.** At this point, your team can choose one of two ways to close the meeting.

    - **Option 1: Prayer Partners.** Get together with your prayer partner and report on your week. Then close in prayer.

    - **Option 2: Circle of Love.** Stay together with your team and express your feelings for each other non-verbally. Here is how. Follow carefully:

        a. Stand in a circle—about a foot apart.
        b. Everyone puts their right hand in front of them—palm up.
        c. Team Leader steps into the circle and goes to one person, looking them in the eyes for a few seconds. The leader then takes that person's hand and tries to express the care he or she feels for this person by doing something to their hand—such as gripping it firmly, stroking it, shaking it ... etc. Use only appropriate gestures.
        d. After the Team Leader has gone around the circle, the next person goes around the circle in the same way, etc. ... until everyone has gone around the circle.

    Remember, all of this is done *without words.*

In shaking the hands of those in your group, you can say a lot— like how you care!

SESSION 7
Life Everlasting

CROWD BREAKER

See *Coach's Book*.

PREPARATION FOR CLOSING

Individual Exercise / 5 minutes

Animal Affirmation. This is the last session in this course. At the end of this session, you will have a chance to evaluate and celebrate what you have experienced. For this celebration, we suggest that you devote five minutes now to prepare for the celebration by letting everyone complete the exercise below. Then, at the end of the session, you will share your choices with the entire group.

Below are a list of animals from a petting zoo. Read over the list; pick one that best describes how you feel about this group. You will not share what you picked until later in this session.

WILD EAGLE: You have helped me discover my spiritual wings and helped me soar like an eagle—spiritually.

LOVABLE HIPPOPOTAMUS: You have helped me clean up my life and get on with it.

SAFARI ELEPHANT: You have helped me get started on the exciting adventure in the Christian life.

COLORFUL PEACOCK: You have helped me see the new person that Christ has made me—something beautiful and special.

PLAYFUL PORPOISE: You have helped me laugh at some of my problems and realize that I am not alone.

OSTRICH IN LOVE: You have helped me get my head out of the sand, enjoy life and have fun.

TOWERING GIRAFFE: You have helped me hold my head up and feel confident about my Christian faith.

ROARING LION: You have helped me stand up for what I believe and speak out for my faith.

DANCING BEAR: You have helped me celebrate life and show my friends that the Christian life can be fun.

ALL-WEATHER DUCK: You have helped me appreciate the storms that I am going through at home and at school.

BIBLE STUDY

Groups of 4 / 15-20 minutes

Night Visitor. The last statement in the Apostles' Creed is: *"I believe in ... life everlasting."*

There are two ways to think of this. This might refer to: (1) the life that begins after we die and go to heaven, or (2) the life that begins now and continues into eternity. In other words, it could be the quality of life, not the place.

The Bible study is about a religious person who came to Jesus to inquire about this life. It is probably the most familiar story in the New Testament—the story of Nicodemus. Nicodemus was a very important person, a leader in the community and a member of a strict religious group that believed in a resurrection and life everlasting. He also knew the Scriptures. This may have been the reason why Jesus referred to the event in the Old Testament when Moses was commanded to lift up a bronze snake to stop a plague. Jesus uses this story to refer to his own death on a cross.

Listen to the story. Then use the questionnaire to discuss the story and share your own experience. This being the last session in this course, save at least 25 minutes at the close to get together and celebrate what you have learned and experienced. Now, move into groups of 4 and listen to the Bible story.

3 Now there was a man of the Pharisees named Nicodemus, a member of the Jewish ruling council. ²He came to Jesus at night and said, "Rabbi, we know you are a teacher who has come from God. For no one could perform the miraculous signs you are doing if God were not with him."

³In reply Jesus declared, "I tell you the truth, no one can see the kingdom of God unless he is born again."

⁴"How can a man be born when he is old?" Nicodemus asked. "Surely he cannot enter a second time into his mother's womb to be born!"

⁵Jesus answered, "I tell you the truth, no one can enter the kingdom of God unless he is born of water and the Spirit. ⁶Flesh gives birth to flesh, but the Spirit gives birth to spirit. ⁷You should not be surprised at my saying, 'You must be born again.' ⁸The wind blows wherever it pleases. You hear its sound, but you cannot tell where it comes from or where it is going. So it is with everyone born of the Spirit."

⁹"How can this be?" Nicodemus asked.

¹⁰"You are Israel's teacher," said Jesus, "and do you not understand these things? ¹¹I tell you the truth, we speak of what we know, and we testify to what we have seen, but still you people do not accept our testimony. ¹²I have spoken to you of earthly things and you do not believe; how then will you believe if I speak of heavenly things? ¹³No one has ever gone into heaven except the one who came from heaven—the Son of Man. ¹⁴Just as Moses lifted up the snake in the desert, so the Son of Man must be lifted up, ¹⁵that everyone who believes in him may have eternal life.

[16]"For God so loved the world that he gave his one and only Son, that whoever believes in him shall not perish but have eternal life. [17]For God did not send his Son into the world to condemn the world, but to save the world through him. [18]Whoever believes in him is not condemned, but whoever does not believe stands condemned already because he has not believed in the name of God's one and only Son. [19]This is the verdict: Light has come into the world, but men loved darkness instead of light because their deeds were evil. [20]Everyone who does evil hates the light, and will not come into the light for fear that his deeds will be exposed. [21]But whoever lives by the truth comes into the light, so that it may be seen plainly that what he has done has been done through God."

John 3:1–21

Looking Into the Story: In groups of 4, let one person answer question #1, the next person question #2, etc. around the group.

1. Why do you think Nicodemus came to Jesus at night?
    - ❒ He didn't want to be seen.
    - ❒ He wanted time with Jesus in private.
    - ❒ He couldn't wait until the morning.
    - ❒ He worked all day.

2. Of the three levels of communication, how did the conversation start out?
    - ❒ mouth to mouth—polite talk
    - ❒ head to head—intellectual stuff
    - ❒ heart to heart—deep sharing

3. What did Jesus mean when he said that one must be "born again" to see the kingdom of God?
    - ❒ You have to be able to point to a specific conversion experience.
    - ❒ Like Bob Dylan said, "He who isn't busy being born, is busy dying."
    - ❒ Our spiritual life has a beginning just like our physical life.
    - ❒ Our spirits are destroyed by sin and they have to be reborn.

4. How do you think Nicodemus came away from this conversation with Jesus?
    - ❒ totally confused
    - ❒ a secret follower of Jesus
    - ❒ convinced in his mind but not in his "heart"
    - ❒ with a lot to think about

My Own Story: Note the shift in sharing instructions. Take question #1 and let everyone answer it. Then, take question #2 and go around again, etc. Remember, to save 25–30 minutes at the close to get back together with your whole group to celebrate.

1. If you were Nicodemus and came to Jesus at night with one question you were a little embarrassed to ask, what would that question be?

2. How would you compare the Christian life in allegories? Choose one in each category.

   life boat _____luxury liner
   trapeze leap _____safety net
   journey   _____destination

3. How would you describe your understanding of the seven statements of the Apostles' Creed now that you have finished this course? Put a dot on the lines.

   GOD: Understanding who God is as Creator and Sustainer of the universe.

   God Who? _____He's Got the Whole World
                                                 in His Hands

   JESUS: Understanding who he is and why he came to be born.

   Nice guy from Nazareth _____Amazing Grace

   HOLY SPIRIT: Understanding who the Spirit is and his role in my life.

   Ghost of_____My Counselor,
   Bible Past   Helper and Conscience

   CHURCH: Understanding what the church is and its purpose.

   It's the Sunday thing_____One in the Family
   to do   of God

   FORGIVENESS OF SIN: Understanding the price God paid for my life and the grace that he offers.

   No Need _____Needed it, love God for it

   RESURRECTION OF THE BODY: Understanding how one day Jesus will come for me to be with him in heaven.

   Couldn't care less _____The driving hope of my life

   LIFE EVERLASTING: Understanding the meaning of new life—both now and forever.

   Don't know, don't care _____Heaven Bound

CARING TIME

LEADER:
Decide whether to use the steps here or the worship service in the *Coach's Book* (or a combination of the two). If you use the steps here you will also need to decide whether to break into the teams of 8 or all stay together.

Groups of 8 or All Together / 25–30 minutes

What Happened? You have two options for this special closing experience: (1) A debriefing session, using the agenda below, or (2) The worship service as described in the *Coach's Book*, Session 7, for the book *Confirmation*.

1. **Affirmation:** Regather as teams (or the entire youth group together) and share the results of the exercise you did on your own at the start of the meeting. Ask one person to share his or her selection and why. Then, move to the next person, etc. around the group. Use this opportunity to share your appreciation for the contributions you have made to each other on the team.

2. **Evaluation:** Go around on each question below and let everyone explain their answer.

   A. When you first started this course, what did you think about it?
   - ❒ I had some reservations. ❒ I liked it.
   - ❒ I only came for the fun.   ❒ I was bored.
   - ❒ other:_____

   B. How would you describe the experience of opening up and sharing your ideas and problems with this group?
   - ❒ scary   ❒ invaluable
   - ❒ very difficult   ❒ okay, but ...
   - ❒ exciting   ❒ just what I needed
   - ❒ a life-changing experience   ❒ a beautiful breakthrough

   C. What was the high point in this program for you?
   - ❒ fun   ❒ times of prayer
   - ❒ finding myself again   ❒ Bible study
   - ❒ knowing I am not alone in my problems
   - ❒ feeling of belonging to others who really care
   - ❒ being with teammates who are committed to Christ
   - ❒ learning to deal with my hang-ups

3. **Personal Change:** Turn back to page 3 and let everyone share one area in which they have changed during this course.

4. **What's Next?** As a group, discuss what you are going to do next. You might decide to do another study. Or perhaps plan a group service project or retreat. For more information contact Serendipity at 1-800-525-9563 *or* via the Internet at: www.serendipityhouse.com.

A Word to the Youth Leaders

Congratulations. You are working with the most potential-packed audience in the world—teenagers. This is one of the most difficult times in their lives. They are making big decisions, often alone or in packs. Peers are important to them and there is tremendous pressure to do what peers demand. This youth program is designed to give teenagers a feeling of belonging. A family of peers. An alternative to the gang at school or the gangs on the streets. Maybe even an alternative inside of the school.

This program is built around the idea of teamwork. The goal is to help youth "bring out the best in one another." By agreeing on a set of goals. By agreeing on a level of commitment for a period of time (seven weeks). By setting ground rules and holding each other accountable. If this sounds like something out of educational psychology, it is. The dynamics are the same. The only difference is the motive and the learning objective. The goal of this program is spiritual formation. Christian orientation. Christian value clarification. Christian moral development. Christian commitment.

The Importance of Voluntary Commitment

The difference between this program and the typical youth program in the church is the commitment level. To get into this program, a youth *must* commit himself or herself to being in the program. This means "choosing" to be in the program every session for seven weeks, to be a team player in order to make the group process work.

Anyone who has been involved in team sports will understand this principle. And anyone who has coached a team will understand the role of the youth leader. The youth leader is the coach and the youth group is the squad. The squad is broken up into small units or teams of six to eight—with an assistant coach or facilitator inside of each team.

Structure of the Youth Meetings

The meetings look like typical training workouts of a sports camp. First, the whole squad meets together for some optional limbering up exercises called Crowd Breakers (all together or by teams of 8 if you have a large youth group). Then, the entire squad pairs off for some basic, one-on-one Conversation Starters to break the ice. Then, with these partners, groups of 4 are formed for the Bible Study discussion. Finally, the team of 8 is regathered for a wrap-up and Caring Time for each other. The typical meeting looks like this:

Step 1: Crowd Breaker / Teams of 8 or all together	**Step 2:** Conversation Starter / Groups of 2	**Step 3:** Bible Study / Groups of 4 or half of team	**Step 4:** Wrap Up and Caring Time / Teams of 8

Moving from the large group (Step 1) to groups of 2 (Step 2) to groups of 4 (Step 3) to groups of 8 (Step 4) will not only offer a spontaneity to the meeting, but will also position the youth to be in the best size group for the particular type of activity.

Step 1:	**Step 2:**	**Step 3:**	**Step 4:**
Purpose: To kick off the meeting	Purpose: To build relationships	Purpose: To discuss Scripture	Purpose: To care for one another

In the first session in this course, the ideal would be to form teams of 8 that can stay together for the entire course. This could be done by random selection or by designating the teams to break up cliques. Or it can be done in a serendipitous fashion by giving out slips of song titles and having the youth find out who is on their team by whistling their song until they "find each other." For junior highs, we recommend that an adult or older youth be in each team of 8.

If you have more than 12 youth, we recommend dividing into teams of 6 to 8 for Step 1 and Step 4. If your group is not more than 12, you may want to keep everyone together for Step 1 and Step 4. At any rate, break into groups of 2 for Step 2 and groups of 4 for Step 3. (If you have less than six youth, you may prefer to stay together for the entire meeting.)

In Case of Emergency, Read the Instructions

In the margin beside each Step, you will find instructions to the leader. Be sure to read them. Sometimes the instructions are very important. Trust us. We have written this program based on our experience. Give the program a chance. There is a method to the madness—particularly the fast-paced movement from 2s to 4s to 8s.

We also recommend using the *Coach's Book* that accompanies this series and is available separately. It includes a game plan and a choice of two Crowd Breakers for every session.

Get a commitment from your youth before you start the program for seven weeks or seven sessions. And remind them of it (by thanking them every week for making this commitment). Here's to what God is about to do in your youth. Here's to the future of your church—your youth.

Serendipity House is a publisher specializing in small groups. Serendipity has been providing training and resources for youth ministry for over 30 years. As we continue to develop materials for youth groups, we would love to hear your comments, ideas or suggestions. Call us at 1-800-525-9563 *or* via the Internet at: www.serendipityhouse.com.

SERENDIPITY HOUSE

SERENDIPITY HOUSE is a publishing house that creates programs like this one for many types of groups in the church: kickoff groups, Bible study groups, support groups, recovery groups and mission/task groups. The philosophy behind these groups is the same: (1) help the group agree upon their purpose and ground rules, (2) spend the first few sessions together getting acquainted, (3) shift gears in Bible study as the group matures, and (4) help the group say "goodbye" and decompress when they are through with their purpose.

ABOUT THE AUTHOR

LYMAN COLEMAN has been a pioneer of the small group movement since the 1950s. During this time he has trained thousands of youth leaders and pastors in the conversation Bible study method through Serendipity seminars. The uniqueness of this series of Bible studies is the group approach to Scripture study—where group building is central in the sharing and caring for one another in a youth group.

Lyman is indebted to the thousands of youth leaders over the years who have helped in the development of the Serendipity youth ministry model. Lyman is especially grateful to Denny Rydberg (President of Young Life), co-author of the first edition of this material, and the Serendipity staff who have worked on this third edition—Matthew Lockhart, Andrew Sloan, Cathy Tardif, Sharon Penington and Erika Tiepel.